# Courage

**Pam Scheunemann**

Consulting Editor
Monica Marx, M.A./Reading Specialist

Published by SandCastle™, an imprint of ABDO Publishing Company, 4940 Viking Drive, Edina, Minnesota 55435.

Credits
Edited by: Pam Price
Curriculum Coordinator: Nancy Tuminelly
Cover and Interior Design and Production: Mighty Media
Photo Credits: Corbis Images, Eyewire Images, PhotoDisc, Rubberball Productions, Stockbyte

Library of Congress Cataloging-in-Publication Data
Scheunemann, Pam, 1955-
   Courage / Pam Scheunemann.
     p. cm. -- (United we stand)
   Includes index.
   Summary: Describes some of the many ways of showing courage, including facing danger in sports, asking for help, and standing up for yourself.
   ISBN 1-57765-877-9
   1. Courage--Juvenile literature. [1. Courage.] I. Title. II. Series.

BJ1533.C8 S37 2002
179'.6--dc21

                                                                2002066401

SandCastle™ books are created by a professional team of educators, reading specialists, and content developers around five essential components that include phonemic awareness, phonics, vocabulary, text comprehension, and fluency. All books are written, reviewed, and leveled for guided reading, early intervention reading, and Accelerated Reader® programs and designed for use in shared, guided, and independent reading and writing activities to support a balanced approach to literacy instruction.

# Let Us Know

After reading the book, SandCastle would like you to tell us your stories about reading. What is your favorite page? Was there something hard that you needed help with? Share the ups and downs of learning to read. We want to hear from you! To get posted on the ABDO Publishing Company Web site, send us email at:

**sandcastle@abdopub.com**

**SandCastle Level: Transitional**

What is courage?

Courage is about being brave.

Sometimes people have to do things they are afraid to do.

It takes courage to do these things.

It takes courage to be a police officer or a fire fighter.

Police officers and fire fighters have the courage to face danger.

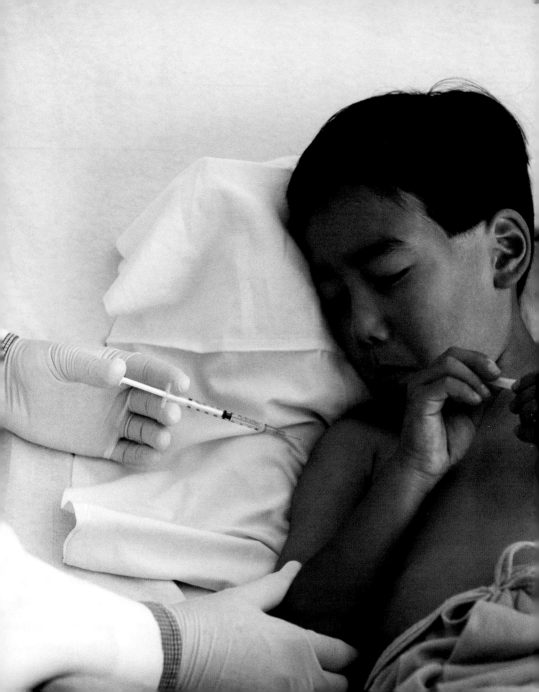

It takes courage to do everyday things, too.

Brian was brave when he got the shot.

It takes courage to ask for help.

Andy was not afraid to ask his teacher for help.

It takes courage to write an answer in front of the whole class.

Ann had the right answer.

It takes courage to play music in front of people.

Lisa was excited about her recital.

It takes courage to learn a new sport.

Pat wanted to be on the baseball team.

Her father helped her to have the courage to join the team.

It takes courage to stand up for yourself.

People do not always agree.

Kate did something wrong.

What helps her to tell the truth?

(courage)

# Index

# Glossary

**agree**    when you share the same feelings or opinions about something

**brave**    having the courage to do difficult things even if you are afraid

**courage**    doing something that is right, even if you are afraid

**danger**    a position that is not safe

**excited**    eager and looking forward to something

**recital**    a musical performance

**truth**    the facts about an act or situation

# About SandCastle™

A professional team of educators, reading specialists, and content developers created the SandCastle™ series to support young readers as they develop reading skills and strategies and increase their general knowledge. The SandCastle™ series has four levels that correspond to early literacy development in young children. The levels are provided to help teachers and parents select the appropriate books for young readers.

**Emerging Readers**
(no flags)

**Beginning Readers**
(1 flag)

**Transitional Readers**
(2 flags)

**Fluent Readers**
(3 flags)

These levels are meant only as a guide. All levels are subject to change.

To see a complete list of SandCastle™ books and other nonfiction titles from ABDO Publishing Company, visit **www.abdopub.com** or contact us at:

4940 Viking Drive, Edina, Minnesota 55435 • 1-800-800-1312 • fax: 1-952-831-1632